also by Emery Allen:

Become.

Soft Human

by Emery Allen

© 2016 Emery Allen

All rights reserved. No part of this book may be used or reproduced in any form without written permission from the author except in the case of brief quotations.

Self published in the USA with international distribution.

ISBN 978-1-329-86654-6

Contact the author at: emeryallen1@gmail.com

last spring, I dreamt that I was at a summer solstice party at my parents' house. I was surrounded by friends that I didn't recognize, but in the moment I knew them. there was a man, but I didn't see his face (I never see his face). he had a lot of rips in his jeans and wherever his skin would show, flowers were there instead. bright ones. we were moving around a lot, in sync with each other. at one point we were all lying on the ground and it looked like we were in a giant bubble. like the whole earth was. when I'd move my head, I'd see the bubble react to the sun and rainbows would wiggle across the sky. I think I was in love with this man. I walked over to my mom, smiling, and she said, *oh, don't be such a soft human.*

vulnerability.openness.compassion.depth.
love.love.love.　　　　　　practice these.

I dreamt of you
before
you came.

find somebody
who will help you
unpack.

you can either become hardened by all that happens to you
or softened.

choose the second. every day.

I want to be immersed
               in the light
      of you.

desire is an empty embrace.
love
and love
and love
is a warm hand
around your throat.

/scene one/

long horizon
gray above,
green below.
an aching river flowing.
there is no anger.
we are in a room with the lights off.
we are in a room with burning embers.
we are warm.
one of your hands is on my face,
fingers curled against my cheek.
we aren't looking at each other
but out the window together.
the river grows wider.
the river cries.
the river moves towards us.
your hand does not move from my face.
we do not look at each other.
you are holding a cigarette in your other hand,
you place the tip in the embers.
you act like the river is not coming.
I act like the river is not coming.
but we both know
it is coming.

dig through the layers
to hear yourself clearly.

no other word
makes my mouth
as tender as
your name.

learn to
mourn
softly
for love.

there will always be new rot in your heart.
pull it out, drop it in the river, forgive.
repeat.

you and I
are standing on different bridges
over the same river.

what a
softness
love
adds to
existence.

I am
learning
to embrace
the void of
you.

you're allowed to mourn
the loss of something
you chose to walk away from.

I miss you
in my dark, dark night. in my
open window. my bare tree.
my morning skin. my rain,
my rain, my rain.

/scene two/

an airport with yellow walls.
an airport that doesn't play music
but the sound of rain,
of crickets.
you are holding a brown bag.
there is nothing in this bag,
you just wanted to see this airport.
you buy a ticket to San Francisco.
everybody in the airport is walking backwards.
you miss your flight
that you didn't come here to go on.
you think this place
is happier
than California.

love

is an accident.

you exist
on this earth.
that fact alone
means you
belong.

your name has transformed
in the back of my mouth.
it is a breath
            that is not mine.

you melt
my longest winter.

fuck the suffering.
did you love?

some people make you softer
just by the way their words sound
when they drip out of their mouths.

I am tender for everybody. my whole being is made up of the tenderness I hold for hundreds of people. some have a freckle on my shoulder or one of the lines in the palm of my hand. I walked by them and they didn't see me, but they were looking at someone like they were in love and that gave me tenderness.
                              but you.
you have my left lung. you have my hip bone that rests under your hand when we sleep. the arches of my feet, the center of my forehead, my shaking knees. I hold the most tenderness for you.

we are all better people
when we are loved.
love others
> as often,
> as wildly,
> as truthfully
> as you can.

you're going to survive your own heart.

if you don't,
that's because you became
prey of heartbreak.
and that is believing you are weak.
and you are not weak.
eat heartbreak for breakfast.
chew it up,
and spit out its grieving bones.

home is alive in you.

in the space that exists
while dying,
the ancient ones
will greet you.
with their big hands,
they will hold you.
you'll sit
in the center of
their palms
and they'll whisper
all of your secrets
back to you.

let me write about
how I'm not going to write about you.
replace your name with whiskey.
replace your name with a clear, silent sky.
replace your name with an unbuilt fire,
a speaker that makes my ears ring,
a road that I won't pass you on.
replace your name with
                      his new hands
                      and his new hands
                      and his new hands.

I have loved you
              in passing.

if they're soft with you
when you mention
the things that
hurt,

let them in.

/scene three/

you are standing
on the middle of the ocean.
blue all around you.
the air is blue.
the water is blue.
the fish are blue.
the fish are coming up to talk to you
but you ignore them.
you think that you are alone
but you just never turn around.
there is a storm coming.
you're watching it from a distance.
you think you'll have to go through it alone
but we're all behind you.
you just never turn around.

love is
bleeding
honey.

your
bee sting
and my
swell.

we cannot deny our suffering.
it is a part of the human experience.
unavoidable and deeply transforming.

being lonely is
the most
human thing
I have ever heard.
be lonely.
want love.
you will find ways
to get through it,
to transform it,
to make it solitude
that is always
welcoming.

/retrograde/
to go back in time.
to walk backwards. run backwards.
to hear you say my name and fall home.
retrograde of the heart, of the soul.
words coming into my mouth.
inhales and inhales and inhales.

you existing
at the same time
as I am
is a miracle
in itself.

I believed in god
when I slept
next to him,
and now
I can't find
anything
to pray to.

how do I stand
in the middle of
unloving
and still
have faith
in love?

you have to dig your way through all of the heavy stuff to find even the smallest amount of light. let that light be what keeps you going until you find the next light and the next. you're going to have a wild collection of light by the time you're all done and you're going to be glad you stuck around for it all.

the aching
poems
can't even
speak
your name.

loving you
would be like
something I'd feel
blessed to
drown in.

if I don't love you right in this life,
find me in the next.
and when you see me for the first time,
                      shake the sky.
                      rain on me,
                      warm and heavy.

we had crashed
together
like waves
of the ocean
and disappeared
into a warm place,
only to
come back
and find each other
again.

everything changes
    when you speak,
your voice
    gives air life.

/scene four/

a very tall room.
a tall door that won't stay shut,
creaks open when the wind blows.
the wind always blows.
two chairs sit in the center of the room.
there is an emerald carpet
underneath the two chairs.
the two chairs are facing each other
but nobody is sitting in the chairs.
they are very close together.
there aren't any windows
but there are mirrors on every wall.
the room is almost all mirror and chair.
you and I
are standing in this room at opposite ends.
I am looking in the mirror at you
looking in the mirror at me.
we are yelling at each other
and not talking about the thing
that will save us.
we yell at each other until we fall asleep
right where we're standing.
when we wake up,
the chairs aren't facing each other anymore.

forever is often quiet and lonely.
wind in the trees.
the things that happen after death
that people pretend to know about.
it doesn't know how to speak,
only touch you with somebody else's hand.

if god is real,
she's a woman
with loud, bloody,
sensual hands.

In the afterlife,
we'll be leaves
that fall next to each other
in a stream.
we'll be mountains,
hands of new lovers,
an early blossom.

love.
even unrequited.
even silent.
even hardly lived.
is better than any vacancy.

unsaid things
don't stay in you forever.
there's a sea of them all
on the other side of dreaming.
there's a sea of them all
where people never go.
nothing swims in this sea,
but it is alive all on its own.
when everything in your world is quiet,
listen hard and you can hear it
humming.

before the womb,
you are a breathing thing
of light -
a stillness
that only exists
in dawn.

the ones who choose fear over love
do not realize that is
a choice that they are making.

I'm glad
that there are small phrases
for such big things.

there would be so little love in life
without second chances.

you are born in the break of a wave.
you are born crying
and you never really learn how to stop.
you carry the sea with you
and hum all of your lovers to sleep -
they wake up tasting
the salt on your neck.

vulnerability will reward you
with love or a lesson.

both will be worth it.

consciously soak in moments.
turn them into movies, into stills.
don't ever forget the seconds
that make life soft and beautiful.
collect them.
review them in your dreams.

to love
is to have
ancient wounds
exposed to
vicious winds
and be caressed
instead of burned.

remain tender
throughout the course of your life.

on the side of a mountain, a small woman sleeps. her dark hair in a thick braid down her back. the soles of her feet glow in the night. each morning she walks to the top of the mountain and then back down, never saying a word. at night she lies in red dirt and dreams. she dreams of you and of me and of everyone we know, everyone we will ever know, everyone we will never know. we are born when she closes her eyes and we die when she opens them, just to be reborn again the next night. some nights she lets me find you. I think the nights when we do not meet I live a little less. when she lets me find you, we love. the sky cries and we love. sometimes I don't recognize you. I don't remember that we've loved before, and those lifetimes are the sweetest because I get to experience you anew all over again. there has never been heaviness when meeting you. some nights she pulls us apart painfully. I know it is to teach us, but I will always want you near. I have lived in many houses and had my bare feet dance against warm wooden floors, but home has never been anything but you. I want to thank this woman, let her rest in my hands.

don't shrink for people.
don't shrink for people.
don't shrink for people.
your soul is an ocean.

/scene five/

a knitted blanket.
a blanket with polka dots.
a blanket that has tassels on it.
more blankets.
a floor of blankets.
a sea of blankets that we are in the middle of.
each blanket has a secret it is trying to tell us
but we can't hear anything.
we are singing very loudly
and our eyes are closed.
it is dark
and I kiss you.
it is dark
and I find your mouth.
we are still singing.
the blankets are still telling secrets.
the sea of blankets is growing.

I want to say that you're
the flesh
my flesh
has been looking for.
I want to put my hands
in the fruit of your heart -
eat it wildly.
devour you
and let the sweetness
drip.

you are not allowed to leave this place.
this place loves you.
this place loves you
even when you feel like it doesn't.
this place loves you
when it gives you heartbreak
because it's handing you
the rest of the world, too.
it's handing you your healing
along with everything else.
you'll see it.
give it time.
keep your eyes open,
even when it's painful.
keep your eyes open and look.

save up your love that keeps flowing.
pour it in jars with honey,
your coat pockets,
used grocery bags,
vases with dried flowers.
keep it safe until
something gentle and alive comes again.

let it hurt
until it doesn't.

/scene six/

a house made of stacked stones.
a house on top of a hill.
the hill is green and alive.
the house is heavy on the hill,
but it is empty.
you are not in this house.
I miss you and you are not in this house.
you are above this house
and I can't see you.
I don't even know you're there.
but you are.
you watch things from this space above the hill.
the sunny days come from you.
the rainy days come from me.
I sit in this house
and wait for you to walk through the door.
I light a candle for you.
it burns.

the only way to get over fear
is to charge straight at it,
to embrace it with open arms
and love what it brings you
when you get out on the other side.

some day the kindness you give out
will come back to you.
maybe not as soon as you'd like,
but it will be here.
threefold, sixfold, tenfold.
your life will be full of *thank you.*
full of *I'm so glad you're alive while I am.*
blossoms everywhere.
love raining down on you.
it will come.

when the pain comes
into you,
you can either allow it to
harden your heart
or
soften it.
it is all
a choice.

solitude.

reflect with yourself.
find what you need
in silence - the
stillness of you.

/scene seven/

it is autumn.
there are no stars. no sun. no moon.
I am on the roof.
I am under a falling golden tree.
the tree is trying to touch me.
I am naked and I am glowing.
you are the falling golden tree.
you have no mouth. no hands.
no way to say /love/.
you are glowing.
I fall asleep
and dream of you having hands,
dream of you having mouth.

be
slow and loving
with your
self.

do not avoid pain.
the depth
it creates within you
is beautiful.
the lessons that come
from it are important.
when you're in it,
it's hard to see it as
anything more
than just pain.
but on your way out,
you're thankful for it.

there is no rush
when it comes to healing.

/ leaving / being left /
creates so much space
for everything else
that is coming.

have hope for things
bigger than what
you presently know.

I have
survived
the loud wars
of my
self.
I can
survive
the ones
you bring
to me.

every day
that passes
is another day
further away
from the things
you want to let go of.
and closer to
the things
that are going to
hold you right.

when are people
ever ready?

learn to jump
with your
eyes closed.

your present suffering
is not permanent.

give yourself permission
to let the painful things go.
drop the memories
that weigh you down
one at a time.
imagine the sunrise
before it rises.
walk into it
like the light
is already there.
it's coming.

surround yourself
with light
or be the light
your surroundings need.

to be gentle,
you must endure
your own
suffering.

sort through the rot
of your heart
and hold it in your hands
until it hurts.
look at it
until you start to understand
why it was in you.
then you must
mend the holes
that it left.

disconnect from who you used to be.
you don't have to carry that person around.

take your power back.
what has happened to you isn't alive anymore.
you own yourself.

embrace the fullness of life
and absence of it as well.
magic lives in everything
and nothing.
magic lives in the space between.

even emptiness
welcomes you.
its hands
are not as cold
as you fear.

writing is
active prayer
to your
self.

/scene eight/

ballroom with a marble floor.
ballroom with a chandelier.
a symphony echoes, unseen.
children line the edge of the room.
some are shy and hiding.
a mountain rests in the center of it all.
a mountain moans.
a mountain reaches inside of himself
and pulls out rocks,
hands them to each child.
they giggle.
he moans.
we stand outside
with our faces pressed against the window,
hands up to block the light.
we say nothing.
he moans.

sit in the center of
the universe
and believe that
everything is right
forever.
it is all right.

when all you can see
is heavy
dig through and
find your light.
/even the
smallest of lights./
collect them
and look
at them often.

always be aware of
the fragility of life.
the breakable beings.
the gone, the going.
love deeply what is here.
let them all know.

the pain in your humanness
will gouge deeply
and you must let it.

/scene nine/

soft blue sky.
cloud dusting.
sun low,
hiding behind a house.
the house is being built slowly.
there is a house across the street
that has been lived in.
now there is no family,
just couches and tables.
these houses have no names.
they watch each other come together
and fall apart.
they love.
they love with abandonment.
love with newness.
love with fear.
these houses would run from each other
if they had legs.
they say this all of the time.
they'd run if they had legs,
to opposite sides of the world.
but they have to watch each other
across the street.
the shadows of each cast over the other.
they stay.

do not minimize pain,
yours or another's.

you can't let yourself believe that
there is nothing you can do to go on.
you have choices.
you always have the choice
to grow or shrink,
to rise above your suffering and go on
or let it swallow you.

                        you can't allow the
                        aching things
                        to win.

the soft center.
dripping and breaking.
only to soften more.
to cry into the next bliss.
to always be open.
always.

believe that you always have choices.
believe that you have the strength
to make those choices,
and the strength to live those choices out.

after you die, you will fall into an ocean. I'm sure it will be storming and I'm sure you'll think you're drowning, but you won't be. you'll forget a lot of yourself, which is okay. you weren't supposed to hang on to it anyways.

you think you can't handle what hurts
and then all of the sudden
you're on the other side of it all,
surviving it.
living beyond it.
and you won't be surprised that you made it.

you will always be shedding past selves.
        always shedding layers.
you are not a solid being.   release.

build a coffin
for each of the selves
that has died.
/do not resuscitate/
decorate the insides
of each coffin with
goodbye letters,
with rose petals,
with a burned match.
bury them in a catacomb,
side by side.
bless them to sleep.
/do not resuscitate/
say a prayer to yourself.
build a shrine
around your bed
to worship the self
that these dead ones
carried you to.

there is always a reason
for your sadness.
you have to dive into that sadness
to find out what it is.

you're going to be so loved. you think what you've felt before them is big, real, right, the only. but oh my god, you're going to be so loved you're not going to know what to do with it all. you're not going to know where to put it all when they hand it to you. you're just going to start giving it to everybody else, smiling at every stranger on the street. all the pennies are going to be facing up for you and you won't even feel like you need to pick them up. you haven't met this person yet but they're there. they're thinking about the person who doesn't want them like they wish they did. they're wondering if that could be it for them. they're stuck like you, neither of you realizing you don't have to be stuck. they're in a bookstore trying to distract themselves from this unrequited thing and a book catches their attention. the only copy, wedged between some others they didn't see at all. it catches their attention and they buy it without even opening it. this is the book you've had next to your bed for three years. the book you carried with you for so long that the colors started changing on the cover, the pages started falling out. they take this book home and set it on the kitchen table, still not opening it. they set it next to an open cereal box and a dirty spoon. it sits there for a long time. they don't open it until they feel like it is time to be somewhere else, like it is time to be a new person. they lay on their couch with a dim lamp behind them, casting a shadow over the pages. they read the whole thing in one night and they don't even sleep. they just watch the sunrise and then go to work. you don't know you're going to love this person yet. you don't know what their hair color is, or what their laugh sounds like drunk at four in the morning. you don't know what gets them to stop feeling sad, you don't know that it's going to be you. you feel the space around you. it's almost loud right now. you can feel it and you can't believe that a person is going to fill it up, quiet it all down. you can't believe that someday a person you haven't met yet is going to take up all of the space in the world. but they're going to. and it's going to be everything that you were looking for. it's going to be everything that this person was not ready to give you.

the first greatest gift of life
is discovering love.
the second is learning that
you can unlove.
life will go on. there is no other way.
you will be okay.
love will find you again.
be gentle with your pain.

you might carry old loves with you
but the heart is always expanding.
and the new love
will grow over the old love.
it is just layers of the soul.

it will stop hurting.
you will grow out of this.
all of this emptiness is going to be filled up.
you've just got to give it time.

my heart
will never
        shout for you.
but it whispers your name
like it's a sacred secret.
like the ancients
placed you here
for me to always
        find you.

either you lose now
or you lose later.
love first.
love and let the possibility
of hurt happen.
otherwise you have
                        nothing.

don't let yourself
be dead in a
breathing body.

nurture
what is now.

it is important for you
to distance yourself
from certain things
for an amount of time
that is necessary
for you to heal.

loving yourself
comes solely from
the insane effort of doing so.
you will find yourself -
but not by
looking in the hearts
of others.

fill all of your time with things
that are kind to you.

/scene ten/

you are walking.
there is snow everywhere.
old snow.
dirty snow.
you are wearing maroon gloves.
an ochre coat from a past life.
a life where you found me and loved me right.
but this life doesn't remember that coat.
you are walking
and I am somewhere else.
you remember me like something
you witnessed in a daze.
you remember me with pieces missing.
the trees lean down.
each one whispers in your ear as you pass,
you are in the wrong place.
run to her.
you are in the wrong place.
this is not for you.
but you can't hear them yet.

poets that write heavily
have lost
and are too aware of it.
poets that write heavily
are missing parts
of themselves
that they don't even
want back.

there is a space between
the breaking
and the reborn.

don't fall in love with your sadness.
let it be something
you kick out in the morning.

/scene eleven/

an oak table on a stone patio.
weeds are growing between the stones.
you are seated at the head of the table,
steak knife in one hand,
fork in the other.
a crystal glass of wine sits next to your plate.
you sip slowly.
the trees towering around you
bow like you're their king.
the world is silent.
my heart rests on your plate.
you eat it like you're starved.
like you can't remember the last time
you had been loved.
bloody mouth.
it didn't hurt at all.

the decay
of old
creates
the blossoms
of new.

slowly take
that love back
and give it to yourself,
to a stranger,
to a best friend,
to people you never really saw
in the first place.

you were never invisible,
but maybe before
you were kinder.
don't break hearts
just to be seen.

> do not fill the void.
> embrace the void.
> make peace with the void.

let this person-shaped hole be a person-shaped hole. live as fully as you can and let the voids just be. spend a lot of time connecting and reconnecting with people. if you're lonely, learn to transform that loneliness into solitude, and then figure out how to be comfortable with these voids.

pain is not pointless.

I think we've all just got to accept that there are holes in us. that we were born full and they appeared over time. that the universe takes things because it needs to. maybe there isn't another reason than that. we spend as much of our lives trying to fill these voids. we won't look at our own and ignore the ones in each other. buy more, drink more, watch more. one day you're going to have to stop pretending they aren't there. if you really want to live, you've got to stop trying to figure out how to make these holes shrink. roll the windows down when you're driving and let the wind blow through them. breathe and the let world keep spinning.

/scene twelve/

a bar lined with lights.
an orange bar.
a bar lined with loud people.
bottles half empty on the shelf.
each one holds a sentence we never said.
"I loved you before I even met you."
"the sky changed when we kissed. stars fell. I took it as a sign of something I never felt brave enough to say out loud."
"you are for me. you are for me."
"now I fall asleep drunk, but I swear alcohol makes the cracks of the heart wider."
"goddamn," the bottle says, *"even in my dreams you're leaving."*
the bottles pour themselves for the strangers.
the strangers cry as they drink.

someday
you're going to have to start
believing you're worthy of love,
and then you're going to have to start
loving.

the truth about love is
you're either very brave
or naive
if you're going to go after it.
the naivety happens once.
everything else that comes after
is bravery.

some things you just need to carry for a while. they're just in you and you can't pull them out. you can ignore them or talk about them all you want, they'll still be in you. you have to grow out of it. make room inside of yourself, make the heart open wider. let them fall out when they fall out.

your love will shrink for people and it will just become soft parts of your past. you carry these people with you always because they were a part of your transformation.
    don't be so afraid to let go.
    there is more love waiting for you.

when I am away from you,
I can feel
the mountains growing
                between us.
I wish to sprout wings
and carry myself
            closer.

I walk backwards
in life
to find you,
knowing that
I am going home.

        you are a soul memory.

imagine what your life would be like if you didn't let go of any of the people you were afraid to let go of.

                    you would be so small.

growth comes from movement, from stepping away from what you know. every person that you had to let go of is pushing you forward by not being there.

/scene thirteen/

a scratched wooden floor.
big windows.
a dainty, round table.
two chairs.
big chairs.
chairs that have stains all over their arms.
ghosts pass outside but never look in.
the chairs howl.
a child, alone,
presses her face against the window
and smiles at the chairs.
daisies appear on the dainty table.
the child shouts something into the distance,
bare hands in the air.
more children appear and look in.
they giggle.
the chairs grow bodies.
bodies that are tall with loud cheekbones.
bodies that have waking hands and love eyes.
the chairs stop howling.
the children dance.
the waking hands reach for each other,
warm and worn.
the tall bodies stand up
and touch each other's faces.
the big chairs sigh.
the tall bodies walk out the door.

dive into your hollowness
and make a home out of it.

master the art of remaining tender.
no hardening of the heart allowed. no walls.
allow everything to make you tender.
let softness inspire softness.

what you're looking for will come. you'll be twenty-one, twenty-four, thirty-six. your hands will look the same as they do now, but with a small scar on your thumb. maybe with calloused fingertips, if you ever pick up your guitar again. you'll have had your first apartment, your first car accident, you will understand how it goes to feel and win, and then to lose. for forty mornings in a row your second thought will be giving up on looking for it. if you were to look back, you'd smile at that. laugh even. your first thought on these mornings won't be a full thought. it will be a hum of clarity with words that aren't invented yet. it will be the residue of a dream. after what you're looking for comes, you'll have invented those words. one night you're going to grab the scissors in your bathroom drawer and cut your hair uneven and shorter than you're used to. you'll look in the mirror with your shirt off, loose hair itching your shoulders. you'll notice one of the lightbulbs has gone out above you, leaving you half illuminated. you tilt your chin up, keeping your eyes locked on yourself. you feel like half a human. a strong half, but still half. your friends laugh at your hair. you don't blush or frown, you just let it grow. when what you're looking for comes, your hair will be how you wanted it to be the first time you cut it. when it comes, you'll have built yourself up. half of you won't be missing. you can thank twenty years for that. thirty years. you can thank every loss and gain, every person that came and left, every book you've lost. you'll have fragments missing but you hardly notice that anymore. you've come so far. when what you're looking for comes, it will fill the small spaces you couldn't find yourself. when what you're looking for comes, you'll exhale.

I hope you never hurt too badly in life.
    I hope the eyes stay gentle.